"Many wo... surpass then... beauty is fleeting; but a woman who fears the Lord is to be praised. Give her the reward she has earned, and let her works bring her praise at the city gate."

Proverbs 31:29-31

To: _____

From: _____

Date: _____

The Power of
MOTHERHOOD

Robert Strand

Evergreen
PRESS

The Power of Motherhood
by Robert Strand
© 2002 Robert Strand

ISBN 1-58169-094-0
For Worldwide Distribution
Printed in the U.S.A.

Evergreen Press
P.O. Box 91011 • Mobile, AL 36691
800-367-8203
E-mail: info@evergreen777.com

TABLE OF CONTENTS

"*A wife of noble character who can find? She is worth far more than rubies.*"

Proverbs 31:10

INTRODUCTION

This is a book written to inspire, encourage, help, and motivate mothers. Over the years, I have come to greatly admire the mothers among us. They are some of the most incredible people walking on the face of this earth. And it goes without saying, but I'm going to say it anyway: without a mother, none of us would have come into this world. You just can't have more importance than that!

A mother is a woman who decorates her world with babies who, if properly nurtured, will grow up to reflect the love she has poured into them. Just perhaps, there will be something within these pages to help her in this process.

Also, I'm interested in encouraging the male population to make a special effort to elevate the mothers among us to their rightful, honored place. Jesus Christ did more to lift women than any other world leader has ever done. He removed all barriers of distinction—race, social status, wealth, or gender—and said we are all one on the same level. Paul the Apostle articulated this concept in many places in his writings, but let one reference suffice: "There is neither Jew nor Greek, slave nor free, male nor female, for you are all one in Christ Jesus (Galatians 3:28). My prayer is that somehow, in some small way, this truth can be further conveyed to mothers as well as their sons and daughters.

My thanks go to all the mothers I have known for being wonderful examples and role models for the rest of us to follow!

I pray that this book will be a blessing to you and to all with whom you might share a copy. The format is purposely designed to be a quick read. Carry it with you to fill some of those spare moments. Pass it on. Perhaps this little book will trigger some family discussions.

Most of all...ENJOY!

Robert J. Strand
Springfield, Missouri
2002

DEDICATION

This book is dedicated to my mother, Ruth Strand Lundeen, who is a living example of all the concepts put forth in this book. Thank you, Mom, for giving me life and the lessons of life, which have been the guideposts for my lifestyle.

"My mother was the most beautiful woman I ever saw. All I am, I owe to my mother."

—George Washington

Chapter One

THE BEAUTY OF LOVE

Several years ago in a tropical country where some Americans were living and working, a terrifying eye disease raged among the children. The American children were the most vulnerable because they lacked the necessary immunity to it. The signs were unmistakable—five days after the first symptoms appeared, the child would go blind. Parents were understandably terrified.

On one particular beautiful morning, one of the American mothers awoke to see all the symptoms of this dread disease in her little girl's eyes. She immediately took her to the doctor only to be told that there was no hope! There was no known medical treatment to stop the disease from destroying the sight of its victims.

Holding back her tears, this mother took her little daughter by the hand and walked with her to a nearby field. The mother picked up her child and again and again, she pointed out the beauties of God's creation to her little one. She showed her how the sunlight lit up the beautiful landscape and how the breeze caused the trees to gracefully sway back and forth. When they knelt among the yellow wildflowers, the mother picked one and held it so her daughter could carefully examine the lovely, delicate structure that only God could make.

Lying down in the field, she cuddled her daughter close and pointed out the fluffy clouds floating overhead in the bright blue sky and the colorful birds in the nearby trees. Spying a bright orange butterfly hovering over a nearby flower, she helped her daughter watch its graceful flight. It was a special time in which the mother did all she could to help her daughter remember the beauty of creation.

She held the little girl up to her face. "Look at me," she whispered gently. "What color is my hair?"

"Black, Mommy. Black and curly and pretty."

"And my eyes...look at them. What color are they?"

"Blue, blue like the sky," she said, patting her mother's face with childish affection.

The mother drew the little girl closer to her breast and held her tightly. Then she looked deeply down into her daughter's eyes. "Now, sweetheart, what do you see in your mother's eyes?"

"Love, Mommy. I see love!"[1]

Knowing that the child's blindness was inevitable, this mother wanted her precious daughter to remember forever what God's most beautiful and wonderful gifts looked like!

For every mother, these bountiful gifts ultimately rest in one's relationship with the Creator. If that relationship means anything to you, and I happen to believe that it does, then you want Him to work through you so that your family can also share in that same relationship, and enjoy the manifestations of God's love—His wondrous creation—that have touched you.

Without a doubt, the most powerful tool in the world that enables us to mold lives is love! Paul the Apostle penned these immortal words: "And now these three remain: faith, hope and love. But the greatest of these is love" (I Corinthians 13:13). If mothers know about anything, they know about love—what it is, how it works, how to share it with children, and how to use it to make a difference in this world.

Jesus Christ challenged us with the task of changing this world through our influence and our lifestyle. The family is God's foundation, the chosen vehicle through which this can be done most effectively. Mother, you *can* make a difference, you *can* make an impact with your love, beginning with your own family!

Thomas Carlyle wrote: "Who is it that loves

me and will love me forever with an affection which no chance, no misery, no crime of mine can do away? It is you, my mother!"

[1] Virgil Hensley, from a fundraising letter, adapted

I Corinthians 13:13

⚡ POWER POINT: What are you doing to share your love with others, particularly your family? Make a short list of specific things you can do that will create lasting memories of your love.

Chapter Two

THE NEED TO BELONG

This is an old story about a little boy, eight years old, who was riding on a city bus alone. He huddled close to a rather well-dressed lady and swung his legs back and forth out into the aisle like kids have a tendency to do. In the process, he accidentally bumped his dirty shoes up against the woman sitting across from him. She became perturbed and asked the lady with whom he was sitting, "Pardon me, but would you please tell your little boy to keep his feet to himself?"

The first lady looked down at the boy as if she hadn't really been aware that he was there. With a nod in his direction, she said, "He's not my boy. I've never seen him before."

Now embarrassed, the little boy moved to another seat, which he attempted to sink into as far down as he could. It was obvious to everyone that he was fighting back tears. He looked at the lady whose dress he had gotten dirty with his shoes and said, "I'm sorry, I didn't mean to get you dirty."

When the woman saw what her reprimand had done to the boy, she began to feel badly and responded, "That's all right. Are you going somewhere alone?"

The boy lowered his head and answered, "I always ride the bus alone. My mommy and daddy are both dead, so I live with my Aunt Margie. But when she gets tired of me, she sends me to Aunt Tillie."

"Are you on your way to visit your Aunt Tillie now?" she gently asked.

"Yes, but Aunt Tillie is hardly ever at home. I hope she's home today because it sure is cold outside," he answered.

The woman looked at the boy again and then said, "You are awfully young to be riding on this bus alone."

He piped right back, "Oh, it's okay. I never get lost, but sometimes I get lonesome. So when I see someone I'd like to belong to, I sit real close and pretend they are my family. That's what I was doing when I got your dress dirty. I just forgot about my feet."

Upon hearing his reply, the woman moved over to where the boy was sitting and put her arm around him. She hugged him closely and put his cold little hands in hers until they came to his stop.

Just like the little boy in the story, we all want to belong to somebody, to be a part of a family, because that is how we have been created. Relationships hold this world together, but they must be worked at. The most successful mothers are the ones who have worked hard to create a feeling of acceptance and security in their children. This security will color their children's future relationships and increase their chances for happiness and success in life.

Ecclesiastes 4:9-12

POWER POINT: Relationships are the core of life. What have you done lately to strengthen your relationships with your children?

*Let every Christian father and mother
understand, when their child is three years old,
that they have done more than half of all
they will ever do for his character.*

Spanish Proverb

Chapter Three

WE ALL WIN

The following story is narrated by an anonymous soccer mom. It demonstrates how one mother had obviously shared her values with her son:

Last night was the last soccer game for my eight-year-old son's soccer team. It was the final quarter. The score was two to one, with my son's team in the lead. Parents shouted encouragement from the sidelines as the boys clashed on the field.

With less than ten seconds remaining, the ball rolled in front of my son's teammate, one Mikey O'Donnel. With shouts of "Kick it!" echoing across the field, Mikey reared back and gave it everything he had. All around me the crowd fell silent as the ball flew into the goal. Mikey O'Donnel had scored!

Mikey had scored all right, but in the wrong

goal...ending the game in a tie. For a moment there was total silence. You see, Mikey has "Down's Syndrome," and for him there is no such thing as a wrong goal. All goals were celebrated by joyous hugs from Mikey. He had even been known to hug opposing players when they scored.

The silence was finally broken when Mikey, his face filled with joy, grabbed my son, hugged him and yelled, "I scored! I scored! Everybody won! Everybody won!" It was the first goal of the entire season that Mikey had made.

For a moment I held my breath, not sure how my son would react. I need not have worried. I watched through tears as my son threw up his hand in the classic high-five salute and started chanting, "Way to go Mikey! Way to go Mikey!"

Within moments, both teams surrounded Mikey, joining in the chant and congratulating him on his goal. Later that night when my daughter asked who had won the soccer game, my son smiled and replied, "It was a tie. Everybody won!"

On reflection, my first thought is what a kind and considerate son, taking into account the feelings of Mikey and helping him celebrate his victory. This mother's son was able to look beyond the immediate to see the really important issue at hand. What a son—a son who would make any mother happy.

But as I think further about this incident, I think about what a wonderful mother this is to have trained her son to react in such a positive, kind, and loving way. How did she do it? When did she start putting this kind of an attitude into such a young head? And who was the mother who trained this mother? Such an ethic of behavior can eventually be traced back to the directives which God has given us. "These are the commands, decrees and laws the Lord your God directed me to teach you to observe in the land...so that you, your children and their children after them may fear the Lord your God as long as you live by keeping all his decrees and commands that I give you, and so that you may enjoy long life" (Deuteronomy 6:1-2).

The parents in the nation of Israel were not only given this command, but God also told them how to carry it out: "These commandments that I give you today are to be upon your hearts. Impress them on your children. Talk about them when you sit at home and when you walk along the road, when you lie down and when you get up...Write them on the doorframes of your houses and on your gates" (Deuteronomy 6:6-7,9).

Imparting directives is a never ending challenge when raising and training children. At some point in life, each child needs to progress enough so that they can make mature judgments and decisions. What satisfaction it is, then, to see your children respond appropriately! When they do, we all win! This is one of the most wonderful of all the joys of motherhood.

Deuteronomy 6:1-2, 6-7, 9

⚡ POWER POINT: Life concepts have been articulated by God in the Bible. Part of parenting is to impart these life principles. What will you do to better implant these into your children?

Chapter Four

ATTITUDE OF LOVE

One of the basic principles of successfully functioning in a relationship is to be supportive. The very best gift that any mother can give her children is to be supportive of her husband. This act teaches far more about relationships than words ever can. Even in situations where the couple is divorced, exchanging mutual respect and support (in most cases) is a priceless example for the children.

The following is one of those warm, wonderful stories about a husband who planned to ask his boss for a sizable raise. He told his wife that, on this particular Friday, he was going into the boss's office to request the raise, which was long overdue and which he felt he justly deserved. Naturally, he was a bit nervous and apprehensive. Toward the end of the working day, he finally mustered the courage to approach his boss with the request he had carefully rehearsed. The words must have come out just right. To his pleasant surprise, the employer readily agreed that he was entitled to the requested increase in salary, and declared that it would be put in place immediately!

When the husband arrived home that evening, he noticed the dining room table was set with their best china, candles were lit, and a floral centerpiece in place. He thought to himself that perhaps someone at the office must have tipped her off with the news of the raise. When he went into the kitchen to tell her the good news, they hugged and kissed, then sat down to the special gourmet meal that she had so lovingly prepared.

Beside his plate was a beautifully hand-lettered note from her which read: "Congratulations, darling! I knew you'd get the raise. These things will tell you just how much I really love you!"

He shared the story of his conversation with the boss as they enjoyed the celebration dinner. They spent time talking about what they would do with the increase of salary.

When his wife went out to the kitchen for the dessert, he noticed a second card fall from her pocket. He bent over, picked it up, and read, "Don't worry about not getting the raise! You deserved it anyway! These things will tell you just how much I really love you!"

What a wonderful, delightful attitude! What an encourager she was! She had thoughtfully prepared for any possibility. What an exciting way to live!

Madeleine L'Engle, in her book, *Walking on Water: Reflections on Faith and Art,* quotes from a French priest: "To love anyone is to hope in him always. From the moment at which we begin to judge anyone, to limit our confidence in him, from the moment at which we identify (pigeon-hole) him, and so reduce him to that, we cease to love him and he ceases to be able to become better. We must dare to love in a world that does not know how to love."

Love is more than an emotion, it's an attitude directed toward another person, motivated by our relationship to Jesus Christ and is given freely without a personal reward in mind! Mothers do it every day. To love their children when they display unlovable traits is a discipline and a decision that is not always easy to follow. But it must be done if children are to learn how to truly love others.

The following are very familiar words but we need to read them often, to burn them into our mind so they become words to live by:

Love is patient, love is kind. It does not envy, it does not boast, it is not proud. It is not rude, it is not self-seeking, it is not easily angered, it keeps no record of wrongs. Love does not delight in evil but rejoices with the truth. It always protects, al-

ways trusts, always hopes, always perseveres. Love never fails" (I Corinthians 13:4-8a).

And what a difference the attitude of love will have on all our human relationships! The Bible challenges us not only to love with our words but with our attitudes and actions! Never forget, the attitude of love never fails!

I Corinthians 13:4-8

⚡ POWER POINT: When you come down to it, there are few things in life over which we have control. Attitude is one of them—it can be controlled and changed. What kind of an attitude do you have toward your spouse and your children? If it's not what it should be, it can be changed!

Chapter Five

THE LAST WORD

A lifetime of demonstrating a loving attitude helped one woman recover from a devastating tragedy. Carol's husband, Jim, was killed in an accident last year. Jim, only 52, was driving home from work, and the other driver was a teenager with a very high blood-alcohol level. Jim died instantly; the teen was in the emergency room less than two hours and his injuries were minor.

There were other ironic twists. It was Carol's 50th birthday, and Jim had two plane tickets to Hawaii in his pocket. He was going to surprise her, but instead, he was killed by a drunken driver.

"How have you survived this?" Carol's friend Debbi finally asked her about a year after the accident had taken place.

Carol's eyes welled up with tears. Debbi was afraid that perhaps the question was not appropriate. But Carol gently reached out and took her hand and replied, "It's all right, Debbi. I want to tell you this. The day I married Jim, I promised I would never let him leave the house in the morning without telling him 'I love you.' He made the same promise. It got to be a joke between us, and as babies came along, it was a hard promise to keep. I remember running down the driveway, saying, 'I love you' through clenched teeth when I was mad. And sometimes I even drove to his office to put a note in his car with the words 'I love you.' It was like a funny challenge for both of us."

They created many lasting memories trying to say, "I love you" before noon every day of their married life. The morning Jim died, he left a birthday card in the kitchen and slipped out to the car. She heard the engine starting, so she raced out and banged on the car window until he rolled it down with a smile. Through the open window she said, "Here on my 50th birthday, Mr. James E. Garret, I, Carol Garret, want to go on record as saying 'I love you!'" What a precious moment in time.

With tears rolling down her face, Carol said to her friend, "And that's how I've survived, Debbi. Knowing that the last words I said to Jim and the last words he said to me were, 'I love you!'" *(Names have been changed.)*

What are the last words that you say to your children when they run out the door in the morning or when they leave for an outing with their friends? How often do you tell them that you love them? Tell them—not just once, but often. Perhaps tonight you can create a special time during your family's favorite meal to express such love to them. Children need this reassurance often. Oh, they may say, "Gosh, Mom, we know that," and look embarrassed, but don't be deceived. It's so important to be loved. They will never forget your taking the time to tell them. This is one of the foundational stones of a successful life.

If you have a problem remembering to do it, why not pray like this: "Lord, today, and every day, remind me to say 'I love you' to my family!" Of course, it's not only to be expressed in words, but it should also be expressed in the actions which precede or follow the words.

It may seem like a simple thing and it is, but it's also oh, so significant. Do you have any idea how many people in our world are dying for lack of love and desperately need someone to express this love to them? The most meaningful way to do so is by saying the words surrounded by the actions which together declare the most powerful, "I love you!"

John 3:16

⚡ POWER POINT: Well…what are you waiting for? There is a line from a Nike™ commercial that says: "Just do it!" Pretty good advice.

Chapter Six

ALWAYS THE TRUTH

Motherhood is a very sacred trust that is based on truth and truthfulness. Children are naturally trusting unless they have been taught otherwise by example.

There is a story about a former President, Grover Cleveland, whose mother insisted on total truthfulness at all times, in all circumstances, regardless of the cost. She modeled it, she taught it, and she, in turn, expected it from him at all times.

Did he pass this test? Early on, while in childhood, he gave proof of the honesty that would later mark him as a man and our future President. As a boy, he insisted upon returning the egg that a neighbor's hen daily laid on the Clevelands' side of the fence. Wouldn't it be refreshing to have such honesty among our politicians today?

Somewhere out there in America are mothers preparing the next generation of national leaders?

Will there be another honest Abe, another Cleveland, another George Washington? There will be if there is a mother who is truthful and who teaches this code of conduct to her children.

Ongoing faithfulness to high principles in the little things will always lead to honesty in matters of much greater importance. This was a major principle of living that Jesus taught about more than once. Be trustworthy in little things and you will be entrusted with greater responsibilities.

Mother, here is another challenge, another principle to live by that should mark all you do and say as you influence your family. Live a life that can stand the daily scrutiny of this test: No deceptions, but always the truth!

Matthew 25:21

⚡ POWER POINT: Have you always been truthful with your kids? If not, now is the time to make that right. Children are enriched when a parent has the courage to admit, "I was wrong. Please forgive me."

Chapter Seven

A MOTHER'S VISION

Talk to almost any seasoned pastor and it seems that all of them have such interesting human interest stories. As seen through the eyes of a clergyman, life experiences are very instructive. The Rev. John D. Walden, Sr. of Lakeland, Florida, is no exception. He has permission to share this story, and I was fascinated by it as he told it:

In a former parish, I met a young Japanese lady named Yoko, who had married an American G.I. and immigrated to this country. She had been attending our worship services with her husband. When their second child, an infant son, died suddenly, I was called to conduct the funeral service.

As a result of hearing a simple Gospel message at the baby's funeral, she accepted Jesus Christ as her personal Savior. Some time later, I asked her to share with me her life story, and I have never forgotten it.

Yoko was reared on one of the northern islands of Japan. Toward the end of World War II, when the Russians began to invade these Pacific islands, her townspeople were fearfully fleeing for their lives. Food supplies were destroyed, and the deprivation and devastation was terrible.

Finally, in desperation, her mother gathered the family and headed down to the harbor to escape. Yoko said the little group consisted of her mother, who carried the youngest child; the grandmother, who was supported by her older sister; and Yoko, who carried her crippled five-year-old brother.

Along the way, they saw many heartwrenching sights of refugees who were also attempting to flee. Some heartless families even went so far as to tie weak, elderly, or handicapped members to poles to prevent them from following and slowing down the progress of the healthy ones.

But Yoko's mother was determined that her family would either survive or die as a unit. No one was going to be left behind. They finally reached the harbor as the last available boat was loading refugees.

Half of the family had managed to get onto the boat when a drunken sailor dropped a rope which prevented any more people from boarding the boat. Already on deck with her mother, Yoko heard her scream, "No! No! We all go or we all stay!" and

23

persuaded the sailor to allow them to disembark and rejoin the rest of the family.

They all stood on the dock, holding onto each other, watching the ship leave the harbor, when the departing ship hit a mine. They heard the explosion and watched in horror as the vessel quickly sank, taking all the passengers and crew with it.

Yoko's father, who was a captain on another ship, was far out in the harbor at the same time this was happening. He was informed of the attempt of the people to evacuate and headed his ship in toward the dock. He arrived just in time to see the ship sink and greatly feared that his family had been on board. What a delight when he found all of his family members safe on the dock where he was able to rescue them.

With tears in her eyes, Yoko concluded her story by saying, "How wonderful that God loved me and was watching over me even before I knew His name!"

I might add how wonderful it was that Yoko also had a mother with a vision for keeping her little family intact. God's love and a mother's love are beyond our understanding! His ways are also far above our thinking, and when mothers draw upon His love, they powerfully touch our lives with it.

Some day, when the curtain has been lifted and we have the privilege of looking back over our life, we will be amazed at the workings of God behind the scenes, through people like our mothers.

The writer of the Psalms points out this obvious truth to us: "Good and upright is the Lord; therefore he instructs sinners in his ways. He guides the humble in what is right and teaches them his way. All the ways of the Lord are loving and faithful..." (Psalm 25:8-10a). That also is the true mission of a mother.

Psalm 25:8-10

⚡ POWER POINT: It's beyond dispute. God is always at work behind the scenes. As you daily make it a point to draw upon His love, your capacity to care for your family will increase by leaps and bounds.

Chapter Eight

KNOWING GOD

Have you ever attempted to explain God to your child? How does a child's young mind grasp the nature of God? How is it possible to get across the idea of a God who is omnipresent, for example? Well here's an eight-year-old's explanation, which was written as an essay for his teacher. The young Danny Dutton wrote:

"One of God's main jobs is making people. He makes these to put in place of the ones that die so there will be enough people to take care of things here on earth. He doesn't make grownups. Just babies. I think because they are smaller and easier to make. That way He doesn't have to take up His valuable time teaching them to talk and walk. He can just leave that up to the mothers and fathers. I think it works out pretty good.

"God's second most important job is listening

to prayers. An awful lot of this goes on, as some people, like preachers and things, pray other times besides bedtime, and Grandpa and Grandma Dutton pray every time they eat (except for snacks). God doesn't have time to listen to the radio or TV on account of this. As He hears everything, not only prayers, there must be a terrible lot of noise going on in His ears, unless He has thought of a way to turn it off. I think we should all be a little quieter.

"God sees everything and hears everything and is everywhere. Which keeps Him pretty busy. So we shouldn't go wasting His time asking for things that aren't important or go over our parents' heads and ask for something they said we couldn't have."[1]

Pretty articulate for an eight-year-old, don't you agree? And yes, it can be an intimidating task explaining the concept of God to children. For example, when do you do it and how do you go about it? How often will you be called on to explain? It seems that at age four they have all the questions and at age 14 they have all the answers. It does complicate the life of a parent somewhat.

However, there is help. The Bible gives us some strong guidelines, or clues, about knowing God. It's also clear that the first steps are to begin when the children are at an early age. (Of course, it begins even before then with your own relationship with God, who commands us to "Love the Lord your God with all your heart and with all your soul and with all your strength" (Deuteronomy 6:5). It begins with you, mom, and how you think about God. If your relationship with God is in good standing, this is a task you will tackle with relish because you want the very best for your children.

The concepts and precepts of God are to be impressed on your children. God says to "Talk about them when you sit at home and when you walk along the road, when you lie down and when you get up. Tie them as symbols on your hands and bind them on your foreheads. Write them on the door-frames of your houses and your gates" (Deuteronomy 6:7-9).

According to this command, it's an on-going task. All of life is to be permeated with the precepts of God. It's also a process of repetition. You do it on an informal as well as a structured, formal basis. So start it young and keep at it constantly—sing to them, read to them, talk to them about God.

Keep the commandments, concepts, and precepts of God constantly in front of your kids. Live it out yourself. Set the example by your attitude and actions. Children will learn by what they are taught but perhaps more by what they have "caught." This is the most valuable teaching you can impart to your kids!

[1] *Calvinist Contact*, from *Men's Life*, October 11, 1985

Deuteronomy 6:5; 7-9

⚡ POWER POINT: The question is: what are you doing about this process of teaching your children about God? Don't give up! Today is the day to get a fresh start. You can do it!

Chapter Nine

JUST SAY "NO!"

Part of teaching our children about God is to teach them His laws. One of the most practical of these for children is the law that says they are to honor their father and mother.

During the American Revolution, an officer was sent through the Virginia countryside to confiscate horses for military use. This was a very normal procedure in those days when there was a desperate need for more animals, equipment, food, or other supplies. They would ask for donations for the cause or simply confiscate them without reimbursing the people by using the right of eminent domain.

One particular officer came to a fine old southern plantation mansion, rang the bell, and asked to speak to the owner. A very dignified elderly lady appeared, and he was invited into the parlor.

He came directly to the point of his visit: "Madam, I am claiming your horses for military use on the orders of my commander."

"Sir," she answered, "you cannot have my horses! I need them now for spring plowing and planting. Who is your commander?"

In full military dress, he stood at attention and replied, "General George Washington, Commander of the American Army, madam."

She replied firmly, but with a slight smile, "You go back and tell General George Washington that his mother says he cannot have any of her horses!"

Wouldn't you have loved to have been there to take in the scene as this officer came back to the camp to report to the General? What do you think was his response? You can be assured that this news must have traveled like wildfire through that military outpost! Mother put her foot down and said a firm "No!" Obviously, this was far from the first time she had ever said "no" to him. It was how she had raised him.

What a wonderful, almost magical, little two letter word this is. Practice saying it. Push your tongue up against the roof of your mouth, give breath to it, practice it, mean it, say it often: "No!"

It's a word that is too seldom used in our society and world. Today, the world says that we are to be politically correct, let people express themselves, and not thwart little minds with the frustrations of a "no." However, in reality, being a mother requires that she not only must sow positive seed in her children but that she must also use the negative command to prevent them from doing wrong.

Respecting the word "no" will pave the way for their eventual success in life because it is the beginning of self-discipline and wisdom. There is a negative as well as a positive side to all of living. When this lesson has been learned, life is much easier.

As General Washington once put it, "I attribute all my success in life to the moral, intellectual and physical education which I received from my mother." In other words, all her "no's" had a significant impact on the outcome of his life, and eventually, the lives of all Americans!

Take the original and first "no." God said to Adam and Eve, "You shall not eat of this tree..." God could have launched into a lengthy spiel about the values and importance of eating from all the trees except the one in the middle. Well, you can see how much simpler it is to say, "Don't eat of this tree."

Mother, there are times when it is extremely important to say "no," mean "no," practice "no," enforce "no," and stand fast in your "no!"

Genesis 2:15-17

⚡ POWER POINT: Have you learned the value of saying "no" to yourself? Are you a disciplined mother? Discipline and the value of "no" are concepts that are caught as well as being taught. You can't teach this to your children until you have learned to say no to yourself.

"My mother said to me,
'If you become a soldier, you'll be a
general; if you become a monk,
you'll end up as the pope.' Instead,
I became a painter and wound
up as Picasso."

—Pablo Picasso

Chapter Ten

POSITIVELY SPEAKING

K eeping themselves from being overly critical is one of those disciplines that mothers must learn if they are to raise healthy, confident children. Here's a story about one affirming mother.

My mom and I recently witnessed a vivid example of this at a fast-food restaurant in our town. A small boy near us hopped down from where he sat with his mother. He ran to drop the remains of his dinner through the swinging lid of a trash can. Rather than returning to his seat, the boy stood there for nearly a minute, his eyes fixed directly ahead. His lips moved silently until he abruptly snapped out of his trance and raced back to his mother.

"Mom," he said, pulling at her coat, "Mom!"

She looked down at him curiously and mumbled, "Hmmmm?"

"I know how to spell garbage!"

"Oh?" She dabbed at the corner of her mouth with a napkin and asked, "How do you spell garbage?"

The boy straightened his spine until he stood at perfect cub-scout attention and announced clearly, "P-U-S...H! And that spells garbage." He grinned triumphantly and anxiously waited for his mother's response.

In seconds, the mother flashed a smile back at her son, reached out, and drew him tightly to her. She kissed him and whispered, "I L-O-V-E you. Know what that spells?" She paused. "That spells what I feel for you!"[1]

What a wonderful insight she had! It's for moments like this that God has created mothers! What a tremendous impact this will have on that particular little boy for time, as well as for eternity!

My wife, who is a counseling psychologist, tells me that every negative remark spoken to a child (or to an adult, for that matter) requires 47 positive affirmations to erase its effects! When dealing with the fragile souls of little people, we must always handle them with care. Not only *what* we say, but *how* we say it to them, is significant.

Think with me, how many of those hurting, cutting, nasty remarks spoken to you do you remember from your childhood? I dare say you can easily recall most of them. Now, can you remember the positive affirmations which have been spoken to you? It's easier to recall the nasty ones, isn't it?

Another thing to consider is that when significant people in a child's life make negative remarks to them, they have much more of an impact than those spoken by strangers. A mother is most often the most significant person to her child. What she says is vitally important, so she, above all others, must be on guard.

It's so easy to destroy children with thoughtless words hastily spoken. Such words are difficult to recall, and the damage is hard to repair. I remind you once more, "A word aptly spoken is like apples of gold in settings of silver" (Proverbs 25:11). The challenge is for mothers to say some exciting, wonderful, uplifting things that can be planted in their children and highly prized. Once more, I draw from the writer of Proverbs, "Gold there is, and rubies in abundance, but lips that speak knowledge are a rare jewel" (Proverbs 20:15).

Mothers, will you make a commitment to set a watch over the words you say, especially to the little ones in your life? Plan on stringing together more of these special moments. What wonderful memories you can build. What an amazing impact you can have in molding a young life. What a challenge! But the dividends are fantastic!

[1] Kerry Setler, *Catholic Digest*, May 1988

POWER POINT: The power of a negative remark is incredible; likewise, the power of a positive expression! Set a monitor on your words. Practice speaking true, noble, right, pure, lovely, admirable, excellent and praiseworthy words, especially to people you love—the significant people in your life. Learn to be a powerful affirmer!

Chapter Eleven

THE JOY OF LIFE

Do you happen to be one of those people who are making too many demands on yourself? Are you one of those who are "driven"? Maybe you are a "type-A" sort of person? Could you be one of those super responsible, I-can-handle-it-all-by-my-self kind of mothers? Or, are you the super-duper, always on the job kind of mother? Is it possible that you are too impatient and too intense? Do you find it difficult to kick back once in a while?

Well, would you at least take the time to slowly read and digest the following? I discovered this little gem of advice written by an anonymous author. That's too bad because somebody should receive the credit for such insight. The author, allegedly, is or was a monk writing from a Nebraska monastery. It's been a help for all of us who need to be a little less tense. I hope this will help you today:

If I had my life to live over again, I'd try to make more mistakes next time.

I would relax and limber up. I would be sillier than I have been this trip.

I know of very few things I would take seriously.

I would take more trips.

I would be crazier.

I would climb more mountains, swim more rivers, and watch more sunsets.

I would do more walking and looking.

I would eat more ice cream and less beans.

I would have more actual troubles and fewer imaginary ones.

You see, I'm one of those people who lives life prophylactically and sensibly, hour after hour, day after day. Oh, I've had my moments, and if I had to do it over again, I'd have more of them. In fact, I'd try to have nothing else, just moments, one after another, instead of living so many years ahead each day.

I've been one of those people who never go anywhere without a thermometer, a hot-water bottle, a gargle, a raincoat, aspirin, and a parachute. If I had to do it over again I would go places, do things, and travel much lighter than I have. If I had my life to live over, I would start barefooted earlier in the spring and stay that way later in the fall. I would ride on more merry-go-rounds, and I'd pick more daisies!

Well said...and I dedicate it to all of us who need a reminder that life is more than a jam packed day-timer. Jesus had some very important things to say about our subject at hand, "Therefore I tell you, do not worry about your life, what you will eat or drink; or about your body, what you will wear. Is not life more important than food, and the body more important than clothes?" (Matthew 6:25)

One more thing—do more than just read about it, put these wonderful words into action in your life.

Matthew 6:25-34

⚡ POWER POINT: Need to slow down a bit? Easier said than done, right? Right! Well, give it a valiant attempt, anyway. Seriously, what is life all about? Take some time to sort out the better from the very best.

"Grandmothers are moms
with lots of frosting!"

—Unknown

Chapter Twelve

LAUGHTER

Laughter is some of the best medicine in life, and certainly something that should be cultivated by mothers everywhere.

A grandmother and her granddaughter, a precocious ten-year-old, were spending an afternoon and evening together, just the two of them. They were busy making supper when the little girl suddenly looked up and asked, "Grandma, how much do you weigh?"

The grandmother was a bit startled, but knowing her granddaughter's quick little mind, she wasn't shocked.

"Well, honey, that's something that you really don't need to know," she replied.

"Awwww, go ahead, Grandma…you can trust me" was her reply.

Feeling a little guilty about being overweight, she wasn't ready to share that information so she ignored the little girl and continued fixing supper. A bit later, she suddenly realized the little darling had been absent for about 20 minutes, which was much too long! She checked around the house for her and found her upstairs in the bedroom. The little girl had dumped the contents of her grandmother's purse on top of the bed and was sitting in the middle of the mess, holding her driver's license.

When their eyes met, the child announced, "Grandma, you weigh 170 pounds!"

"Why, yes, I do. How do you know that?"

"I found it here on your driver's license!"

"That's right, sweetheart. Your grandmother does weigh that much.""

The little girl continued to stare at the driver's license and solemnly added, "You also made an 'F' in sex, Grandma."

Joy, humor and laughter will release some of the tensions in your life. Refusing to let the difficulties of life dominate your day-to-day attitude will help you to enjoy life a bit more and make it more stress free. In doing so, you will gain a new perspective and look at life through the eyes of a child once more. Give yourself permission to laugh again!

Are you aware that, on average, according to studies, kids laugh about 150 times each day, but adults laugh only about ten times! What's happening to us, adults? We have a laughter famine!

To laugh is to chuckle, giggle, roar, chortle, guffaw, snicker, titter, cackle, break up, roll on the floor, howl, and to split one's side. I hope that all of the above is part of your life experience every day or at least will be.

Does God laugh?

Well, in the Bible, you will find the word "joy" appears in some form more than 200 times! The word "rejoice" is found 248 times! The word "laugh" or "laughter" is penned some 40 times! Yes, God does laugh! Consider Psalm 2:4, "The One enthroned in heaven laughs!" Or again, Psalm 37:13, "The Lord laughs at the wicked, for He knows their day is coming." To laugh and to be joyful is a choice!

Somewhere between childhood innocence and advanced adulthood, life has become too grim! When did a well exercised sense of humor and joy get sacrificed on the altar of adulthood? Who says that being a Christian means putting on a long face?

Here's a laugh prescription by Dr. William Fry, psychiatrist at Stanford University Medical School, who writes: "Laugh 100 times a day and you may feel like an idiot but you'll be in great shape. In fact, you'll have given your heart the same workout you'd get if you pedaled on a stationary bike for 15 minutes. Over time, chuckling this much also lowers blood pressure and heart rate, reduces pain, strengthens the immune system and cuts down on stress-creating hormones. The biggest problem is finding that many things to laugh about!"

Need more encouragement to laugh and be joyful? "A cheerful heart is good medicine, but a crushed spirit dries up the bones" (Proverbs 17:22).

Psalm 2:4; 37:13; Proverbs 17:22

⚡ POWER POINT: Laughter and other expressions of joy are necessary ingredients to making a house a home. What are you doing to make life more enjoyable for yourself and those around you? Try writing out your own laughter prescription and have fun!

Chapter Thirteen

FLEXIBILITY

The following mother had to dig deep to let her funny bone be tickled in the following story.

"Things are not always as they seem! It was late in the afternoon in the crowded shopping mall. My three-year-old daughter and I had visited almost every store. I could tell she was getting tired of browsing and shopping, from her comments of 'When are we going to go home?'

"To counter her growing discontent so I could finish my shopping, I asked her if she would like to visit the toy store just ahead. She responded with a squeal and took off in the direction of the toy store as fast as her little feet could carry her. I broke into a trot to catch up to her. Just as I got within two feet of her I teased, 'I'm going to beat you to the store.'

"Looking back over her shoulder, she saw me

gaining on her and unexpectedly yelled at the top of her lungs, 'Don't beat me, Mommy! Don't beat me!'

"All of a sudden, I looked around and realized that everyone in that area of the mall was watching this scene of a mother chasing her small toddler who was yelling, 'Don't beat me, Mommy!'

"Embarrassed, I yelled back to my daughter, 'Don't worry honey, I'll let you win our little race. I won't beat you.'

"Somehow, judging from the looks on the spectators faces, I don't think they believed me."[1]

Children, big or little, how delightful they can be! But the things they say can be embarrassing at times. So what kind of a life application will this fun little story lead us into, today?

Quick thinking, innovativeness, developing a sense of humor, enjoying change, and going with the flow are just a few that come to mind. These are the qualities that every mother needs, maybe not all the time, but when the occasion calls for it. How do you cultivate these kinds of life skills? Unfortunately, I could find no easy formulas. But in my humble opinion, I believe these qualities spring from an attitude of flexibility. Not everything in life turns out just right. Not every day will go as planned. Not every relationship will always go smoothly.

However, the following is a biblical guideline

to live by in dealing with such situations: "Be joyful always; pray continually; give thanks in all circumstances, for this is God's will for you in Christ Jesus" (I Thessalonians 5:16-18). There's one thing to carefully note about this admonition. It doesn't say "give thanks *for* all circumstances" but it does say "*in* all circumstances." A small difference, but a large one when you are faced with trying circumstances. The one thing you must be careful about is that you never are caught "under" the circumstances!

So let's have a Strand paraphrase: "Blessed are the quick thinking, for they shall survive many or most all of life's little surprises!" We hope! So, today, think about survival, quick reactions and flexibility. Have a "flexible" kind of a day!

[1] Kim J. Wilson, THE PASTOR'S STORY FILE, May 1990, pg 3

I Thessalonians 5:16-18

⚡ POWER POINT: Mother, loosen up a bit. Not everything will turn out just right. Flexibility is the keyword to the power of enjoying family life.

Chapter Fourteen

CELEBRATING MOTHERHOOD

Something strange began happening to me when I became a father for the first time many years ago—I also became a champion of women! I had been raised in a family of three boys but had no sisters. So, when the impact of my children, and especially a baby girl, came into my life, something changed. I began to be a bit angry at a world which was so insensitive to my little girl, as well as the other women in my life. In fact, it made me angry enough to attempt to want to do something about it.

The first thing I had to do was to work on my own attitude and conduct towards females. (And I must confess that I still am a work in progress.) Somehow, the women among us are taught that they are to be some kind of second class citizens when it comes to many things in our society. Look what others nations are doing to their women, too. So first, I had to scrutinize my attitude and deliberately change it.

Another aspect began to come into play—I began to serve as a pastor and had some influence in the lives of others and could make some changes where possible. I made it a point to hire female staff members, attempting to equally divide my ministry staff, if at all possible, between male and female, because I felt this was a powerful statement about how life should be lived. For example, I always considered my wife to be an equal in our life and ministry together. I tried to influence my family and my congregation, and in my small way, make a societal impact. It is fun and still a learning experience.

But every year when I began planning a special "Mother's Day" celebration in the church, I would always feel frustrated. Oh, there were lots of biblical examples of wonderful, exciting and powerful women to use as sermon material—Naomi, Ruth, Miriam, Esther, Mary Magdalene, and Lydia, just to name a few. But what about some fitting music for the occasion? I searched diligently through our church's hymnals, in vain I might add, to find a hymn which thanked God for our "fore-mothers" in the faith! There are lots of hymns which are dedicated to our "fore-fathers" but nothing for mothers.

Now, here is a niche in hymnology which

someone needs to fill! We attempted substituting key words to "Faith of our Fathers" to "Faith of our Mothers" but that was feeble at best.

However, in my research I came across words penned by Rev. Barry Bence of Canada, who had much the same problem as I had, but he was more creative and wrote his own hymn for mothers. If you are musically inclined, this hymn is sung to the tune of "A Mighty Fortress." The good Reverend states that "any church who wishes to sing it in a service of worship is more than welcome to find the music and share these words." So, mother, on your day, your family and your church can join in singing the following:

Praise God whose love shines warm and bright
    in every woman's caring,
Whose heartbeat throbs for all the world
    in every woman's daring.
Our mother, daughter, wife,
    are fountains of your life…
In Christ our sisters, too,
    are daughters unto you!

Praise Christ once born of woman!
You made a man of earth's red clay
    to tend and guard creation,
The woman shaped that primal day
    to bring forth earth's redemption!

Our partner to life's end,
    our teacher, lover, friend,
Bless all your daughters who,
    like Mary, cradle you,
Whose grace is of the Spirit.
                    —*Barry Bence*

Well, what do you think? A bit schmaltzy? Yes, but what's wrong with expressing to God our thankfulness for the precious women in our lives?

Galatians 3:28-29

⚡ POWER POINT: All together now, let's sing! And if you're brave, you could share this chapter with your sons or spouse or other male friends. But be gentle about it.

"A mother is a person who,
seeing there are only four pieces
of pie for five people, promptly
announces she never did care for pie."

—Tenneva Jordan

Chapter Fifteen

A MOTHER'S VALUE

Sylvia Porter, the noted financial analyst and writer, states that 25 million full-time homemakers contribute billions of dollars to the economy each year, even though their labor is not counted in the GNP (Gross National Product).

Porter says only the wealthiest of families could pay for the services a mother provides out of love. She calculated how much the mother added to her family's economic well-being by assigning an hourly fee for the various duties such as: nursemaid, housekeeper, cook, dishwasher, laundress, food buyer, chauffeur, gardener, maintenance person, seamstress, dietician and practical nurse. She found that the labor performed by a mother at home would cost the family approximately $34,580 if they lived in Greensboro, South Carolina; $37,962 if they lived in Los Angeles, California; and $39,735 if they resided in Chicago, Illinois!

Today, many women also work outside the home and so carry even more responsibility. In a major sense, this analysis is demeaning to all mothers, because Sylvia Porter only looked at the relatively menial duties. She did not consider the higher status jobs every mother performs such as: teacher, coach, interior decorator, religious education instructor, values clarifier, vision setter, mediator, tutor, manager, motivator, counselor and child psychologist, to name only a few!

"Your government should give you a medal for productivity," said Porter to mothers. "Your family should appreciate and cherish you." Indeed! Let's hear it for moms!

Mothers are one of today's unsung heroines! Yes, she provides some very pricey services which cannot be duplicated by any other person. Where would you find a substitute for a mother? How could you get anybody else to do the work of a mother? Certainly, not too many men could fill the bill!

Remember, what happens in the home affects what happens in the church, the school, and the workplace. All we have to do to see this in action is to observe what is going on in our world.

The following poem written by an unknown author captures a bit of what I've been attempting to say:

Every time I put my pajamas on, it gets dark.
Every time the phone rings,
I have this urge to make noise.
Every time I go to bed, I need a drink of water.
Every time I get a drink of water,
I need to go to the bathroom.
Every time I need a friend,
My mom is always there!

So, mothers, please accept our thanks for a job well done! You are highly valued—you are priceless!

There's an old Spanish proverb which states: "God couldn't be everywhere so He made mothers!"

Proverbs 31:10-31

⚡ POWER POINT: Mother, are you a bit discouraged with your life situation? Just for today, give yourself a pat on the back. Just for today, think of your worth to your family and society. If you can do it for today, how about carrying this thought with you the rest of your busy life?

Chapter Sixteen

IN A MOTHER'S GARDEN

ONCE UPON A TIME, long ago and far way, there was a gardener. She was an excellent gardener who paid special attention to every one of her plants. As a result, her garden always flourished.

In the springtime, she always carefully prepared the soil for the seed. The soil was turned over and over to separate out all the weeds and rocks. Then she tilled in fertilizer and compost until it was ready for planting.

However, each season of the year brought new challenges, so she attended neighborhood meetings where gardening tips were generously shared. During one such meeting, her fellow gardeners recommended leaving the soil just as it was found. They said, "The plants would grow stronger if they struggled in hard soil!" They thought she was crazy for spending so much time preparing the soil. Her philosophy was, "Why, it should be good enough for them to have comfortable beds to stretch out their roots."

Summer came, and with it the harsh sun which threatened to dry up both soil and plants. She carefully set up a drip irrigation system for her young plants. However, her fellow gardeners criticized her for being "over protective."

Fall arrived and the good gardener had a bountiful harvest. Each plant grew strong and tall. Her fellow gardeners harvested little, and what was harvested appeared weak and disease-infested.

Therefore, hear the Parable of the Good Gardener as you grow your garden and raise your children.[1]

To "nurture" has the meaning of "feed, nourish, foster, tend, sustain, maintain, strengthen, train, discipline, develop, prepare, cultivate, tutor, school, educate, teach, instruct, bring up, rear and raise." This is quite a word with strong meaning; simple to understand but tough to do.

Nurturing is an essential element in the responsibility of being a mother. For children, maturity doesn't come easily, quickly, or without somebody nurturing them. To help children develop into mature human beings is an ongoing and continuing educational responsibility of a mother. It's more than birthing children. Parents are to be involved in raising their children until they come to a place of maturity where they can become responsible for themselves. This is a simple way of stating what maturity is—being responsible for ourselves and our decisions.

This responsibility to nurture requires a partnership with your spouse as well as with your God. After all, the process of birth and growth is His concept and He works with parents who work with Him. There are commands and there are rewards of mothering. Nothing can be more exciting than observing young people mature and become productive citizens in God's world!

The book of Proverbs is crammed with instructions such as this one, "Listen, my son, to your father's instruction and do not forsake your mother's teaching. They will be a garland to grace your head and a chain to adorn your neck" (Proverbs 1:8-9).

[1] Keith Knauf

Proverbs 1:8-9

⚡ POWER POINT: Think about some specific ways in which you could improve the nurturing process within your family.

Chapter Seventeen

GIFTS THAT ENDURE

Are you the type of mom who loves to give gifts to her children? Of course you are. Sometimes you feel bad that you can't fulfill one of their wishes. More important than anything you can ever buy them are the gifts that will last with them for a lifetime. The following are some of them:

1) **The gift of listening**: This is probably one of the most valuable of gifts you can ever give them. This means not interrupting and no daydreaming or planning your responses. Just be there and listen! You will be amazed at the dividends this gift will pay back to you.

2) **The gift of affection**: Learn to be generous with your hugs, kisses, and gentle squeezes. Let these actions demonstrate the love that is on the inside.

Maybe it's just a pat on the top of a little head, but it doesn't take much, sometimes, when the object of your affection can really feel that you love them.

3) **The gift of a note**: It could be as simple as an "I love you" note put in a school lunch, or as creative as a poem you frame for their room. They mean even more when they're least expected, too. Make it a surprise and they'll never forget it.

4) **The gift of laughter**: Have you ever thought of sharing a humorous cartoon? Cut it out and give it to a son who would chuckle over it or a daughter who needs a little pick-me-up. Keep that clever article you came across and pass it on. Share a good joke when you find one. Put a humorous card on their dresser. This gift will say, "I love to laugh with you!"

5) **The gift of a compliment**: A simple "You look great today!" Or "I like your hair fixed like that." Or, "Thanks, honey, for the help." Or, "Thanks, son/daughter, your room looks great today." You can think of many compliments, so be creative. Some of these will be treasured for a lifetime. Kind words are especially effective when someone feels left out.

6) **The gift of a favor**: Let's think a moment.

Which child is in need of a favor, a helping hand, or someone to lift part of their load? How about helping with their chores or doing their paper route for them when they have a lot of homework or several tests the next day?

7) **The gift of being left alone**: There are times in life when we want nothing better than to be left alone to have some quality time by ourselves. Sometimes your children may need your consideration in offering this gift, especially as they become older. Be sensitive to those whom you love and give this gift when needed.

8) **The gift of a cheerful disposition**: How about trying to be a bit more cheerful around the house? Maybe your child's day hasn't gone well. Perhaps they have had a problem with a friend. A word designed to lift their spirits would be appropriate. Give this gift often to the people whom you love.

9) **The gift of a game**: Offer to play a game with your child. Be patient, it may take twice as long for them make their move than for you, but it's worth it to spend time doing what they enjoying doing.

10) **The gift of prayer**: Pray for your children during the day and let them know you are doing it. Praying for someone is a way of saying, "You are so

special to me that I'll talk to God about you and on your behalf." A praying mother is a powerful one!

Proverbs 25:11-13

POWER POINT: There is a tendency for us to want to complicate life. Keep these simple suggestions in the back of your mind to use whenever appropriate. Giving from the heart is what makes the difference.

Chapter Eighteen

TAKING RESPONSIBILITY

The following is an old story set in a small village in the foothills of the French Alps:

The town doctor was about to retire. For many years, he had given himself in unselfish service and ministry to care for this humble village and all its inhabitants. As the day of his retirement approached, the people decided to make an expression of their gratitude and affection to the good doctor. Since they had little money to give, it was finally proposed that on a given day, each family was to bring some wine from their own personal cellar and pour it into a large barrel in the village square. This barrel of wine would then be presented to the doctor as a token of their expression of love.

It was a festive and happy day. The barrel was finally completely filled after all the families had taken a turn pouring in their gift of wine. With much pomp and ceremony, the barrel was paraded to the good doctor's home by all the villagers. The presentation was made with many speeches of endearment and expressions of thanks. The doctor and his wife returned their thanks and gratitude. It was a wonderful time they all shared together. It ended with a long and loud applause, warmly given, and smiles and hugs exchanged.

The villagers finally departed, leaving the doctor and his wife alone in the glow of the town's expressed love. Glasses in hand, the happy couple drew off a bit of this special blend of wine and proceeded to sit by the fire and enjoy it.

The first sip was a shock! It tasted like water! They sipped again and looked at each other in astonishment. It *was* water! They went back to the barrel to draw more off, thinking there must have been some kind of mistake. But no, the barrel was entirely filled with water! The truth dawned on them. Each of the villagers had reasoned: "My contribution of wine won't be missed. Others will take care of it. The little water I am substituting for the real stuff will never be noticed!"

And so, they turned wine into water!

It's a tragic little story and may never have really happened. It may be one of those legends, based perhaps on a real incident, but the truth of the story hasn't changed. It's a life lesson that showcases the reasoning of too many people when it comes to taking responsibility: "Let somebody else do it! I'll just pretend I'm going through the motions."

Mother, your contributions are important to your family, neighborhood, community, church and the kingdom of God. You do have the power to turn the wine of hope or vision into nothing! Or, you can accept the responsibility to do the right thing even when nobody is watching. The Bible places a premium upon being faithful, consistent, and responsible in little things, because a reward and a promotion are sure to follow, "Well done, good and faithful servant! You have been faithful with a few things; I will put you in charge of many things. Come and share your master's happiness!" (Matthew 25:21)

The life principle is quite simple—be responsible in little things, and you will be rewarded with larger ones. This concept has an application in all areas of living but especially in nurturing the little ones placed in our care.

What will it be? Wine into water or water into wine?

Matthew 25:21

 POWER POINT: No one can be responsible in your place. No one can be a caregiver where you are the one is supposed to be responsible. What will you do to exhibit this life characteristic in your current circumstances?

Chapter Nineteen

FEAR NOT

The following story took place in one of the Nazi concentration camps during World War II:

The Rosenberg family had been imprisoned in a particular work camp where the gas ovens could be avoided as long as a person could work a full day.

Grandpa Rosenberg and his wife, well into their 80s, did not long survive the horrible hours, lack of decent food, and miserable hygienic conditions. They were soon sent to their deaths.

The next generation of Rosenbergs—Solomon and his wife—had their two sons with them in the camp. Because the younger one, David, was partially handicapped, Solomon feared that he would surely be the next one to go to the ovens.

Every morning, the family was separated for

their work assignments, and every night, they returned to huddle together in the barracks. Each day, Solomon wondered if it would be the day when David would be taken. As he entered the barracks each night, his eyes quickly sought out his family.

At last, the night came that Solomon had feared. When he walked into the barracks, he could not find his family and became frantic. His eyes searched again for their precious faces when, at last, he saw the figure of his oldest son, Jacob, hunched over in the corner, weeping.

Solomon hurried to Jacob, "Son, tell me it isn't so. Did they take David today?"

"Yes, Papa. Today they came to take David," he said sadly. "They said he could no longer do his work."

"But, Mama, where is Mama? She is still strong. Surely they didn't take Mama, too?" he asked.

Jacob looked at his father through tear-filled eyes and said, "Papa, Papa. When they came to take David, he was afraid. And he cried. And so Mama said to David, 'Don't cry, David, I will go with you and hold you close.' Mama went with him to the ovens so he wouldn't be afraid."

What a heart-wrenching story of commitment and love. God's kind of love—a mother's kind of love—is to be able to say, "I will go with you and hold you close." One of the things God does for all of His children is to calm our fears. I've been told that the Bible has recorded the words "fear not" at least 365 times, one for every day of the year.

God has promised to be with you, mother, no matter what kind of days are ahead for you! He's promised never to leave nor forsake you. And He has promised to hold you close, so you needn't be afraid.

The promises are powerful and numerous. For example: "Do not fear, for I am with you; do not be dismayed, for I am your God. I will strengthen you and help you; I will uphold you with my righteous right hand.... For I am the Lord, your God, who takes hold of your right hand and says to you, Do not fear; I will help you," (Isaiah 41:10,13).

With such promises, the everyday challenges of motherhood can be handled, one day at a time.

Isaiah 41:10, 13

POWER POINT: The love of God is beyond understanding. It's a constant. It's the pattern for a mother's love. Mother, in your life journey, trust in that God of love—His promises are positive and sure. You can make it with that help. Perhaps this is your moment to give Him praise and thanksgiving for His help in your life.

"Mama was my greatest teacher, a teacher
of compassion, love and fearlessness.
If love is sweet as a flower, then my mother
is that sweet flower of love."

—Stevie Wonder

Chapter Twenty

GOING THE LAST MILE

Perhaps you have read the books of Peter and Barbara Jenkins: *Walk Across America* and *The Walk West: A Walk Across America 2*. If you haven't, I recommend that you find the books and read them. They are true life odysseys and both contain wonderful stories told by great storytellers.

Peter began the journey alone, as he walked with his dog from New York State down to New Orleans. There he met his future wife, Barbara. They married and together took up the trek, heading northwest across Texas, New Mexico, Idaho, Utah, and Oregon up to the Pacific Coast.

When they were nearing the end of their journey, they wrote to many people who had befriended them along the way. They invited them to meet them in Florence, Oregon, to walk the last mile and celebrate the completion of their remarkable feat. One of those who joined them was

Barbara's 83-year-old grandmother. She led them and all those who had joined for this last mile. As she did, she also sang. Let's pick it up from the book:

"Her voice was squeaky and high but sounded sweet to me as the slapping ocean waves that were just over the ridge ahead of us. Grandma's eighty-three-year-old hands were wrinkled, little and frail, but she held to us with a tight grip, walking in brisk steps. She wasn't even five feet tall and weighed a light eighty-five pounds, but her tiny steps led the way, setting the pace for all of our friends behind us."

As they came over the top of the dunes Barbara's grandmother led them in singing the old church hymn, "The Last Mile of the Way":

If I walk in the pathway of duty,
If I work till the close of the day,
I shall see the great King in His beauty
When I've gone the last mile of the way.

They came over the last sand dune and there was the Pacific Ocean spread out before them. Peter writes:

"Barbara and I broke from the rest. There was

only fifty yards of beach left and then the ocean. We couldn't stop; we walked into the Pacific. We held our hands up. I was crying. If all that I felt could have come out of me, I don't think I could have expressed it. The water may have been cold; a wave hit us and almost knocked us over. It may have knocked some of the others over. I reached for Barbara; we hugged because we had to share some of this moment in the surf. There was no land left to walk. I was glad it was over and I was sad. What this walk meant to me would take a lifetime to understand."

Do the circumstances of life seem to be keeping you from attaining your goals? Do you feel like giving up on your children? Do you find yourself in a titanic kind of struggle with them? Ever just want to throw in the towel? Yes! Absolutely. Haven't we all at times? It's quite human to struggle, and there are times when victory seems so far out of reach that it would be easier to give up than to persist.

Being a mother is something that never ends. Don't be discouraged when it seems as though problems are mushrooming around you faster than you can handle them. Remember, this too shall pass. It won't be long and your children will be off to school, teenagers, or even married. What you do with the time you have now with them is extremely important. Don't give up when you think they never listen to you. Remember, what you are trying to teach and nurture in them is something that will last a lifetime, so don't be in a hurry.

Persistence has been described as the process of putting one foot in front of the other in spite of how hard it may be. Here is a special prayer for you in your motherly persistence: "We pray this in order that you may live a life worthy of the Lord and may please him in every way: bearing fruit in every good work, growing in the knowledge of God, being strengthened with all power according to his glorious might so that you may have great endurance and patience... (Colossians 1:10-11).

Colossians 1:10-11

⚡ POWER POINT: Persistence is a mind set before it translates into life actions. It's strengthened by exercise, by being persistent and hanging in there. It's refusing to give up when the going gets tough. Ultimately, the strength for persistence comes out of God's strength—that's the power invested in mothers.

Chapter Twenty-One

A MOTHER'S HAND

The events of September 11, 2001 will be forever etched in the minds, souls, and hearts of all Americans. They have changed us in ways we never thought possible. Time has passed since this horrible terrorist attack, but our minds are still haunted by those appalling images of exploding airliners, collapsing towers, and mourning families. Out of this rubble of broken lives are coming many stories of special people and their acts of heroism. This is such a story about a wonderful mother:

None of Dora Menchac's family or friends have to wonder how this 45-year-old clinical researcher from Santa Monica, California, likely spent her last minutes of life aboard the ill-fated American Airlines Flight 77, the airliner which crashed in the countryside of Pennsylvania.

Dora was known as the "proverbial therapist's

couch." She was the person with whom others confided their troubles and secrets. She was a relentless professional.

The daughter of Mexican immigrants, Dora left behind a husband, four-year-old son, and an 18-year-old daughter. When a business meeting had been cancelled, she hurried to catch an earlier flight home because she wanted extra time with her family and to spend in her garden.

Flight 77 was the result of this choice—a flight which was re-routed by terrorists who intended to crash it into one of the buildings in Washington, D.C., possibly the White House or the Capitol building, who knows.

Mary Ann Foote, Dora's fellow researcher said, "She was the mother figure. I have no doubt that Dora had someone's hand in both of hers when the plane went down."[1]

The after-shocks of this horrible act are still with us. What's a mother to do for her children when something of this magnitude occurs? According to Tamar Chansky, Ph.D., who is the director of the Children's Center for OCD and Anxiety wrote: "Parents should continue to maintain normal routines, providing a sense of structure and balance for kids, even while allowing them to express their feelings about September 11."

In a survey taken six months following 9/11, 45% of the parents interviewed said that their children were affected by it in one way or another. This is a wonderful opportunity for mothers to help their children to experience the security and safety we have in our relationship with Jesus Christ. It's a time to share the comforting promises of God's Word, promises such as the one found in Isaiah 40-41. It's a time to take a child into your arms and pray with them about their future and reassure them of your love for them. It's a time to teach valuable lessons about praying for others who may be hurting because of their losses. It's a time to encourage them to pray for our president, his advisors, and our congressional leaders to make the right decisions as they seek to protect our country from suffering such losses again.

Mothers have a God-given opportunity to use whatever is happening in their children's lives and the larger world around them as a basis for teaching them valuable principles and lessons in life.

[1] Adapted from *U.S. News and World Report*, Sept. 24, 2002

Romans 8:35-39

⚡ POWER POINT: Yes, the events of 9/11 have forever changed the way we will live in the future. As we urge caution, let us not withdraw from life. This is the time to reaffirm to our children the protection and care which God gives us. Yes, bad things can happen to good people, but help your children to overcome their fears and learn to trust ever more in their heavenly Father.

Chapter Twenty-Two

TWO LAST WORDS: "KEEP PLAYING!"

A mother, wishing to encourage her young son's progress at the piano, bought tickets for a Paderewski performance. When the night arrived, they found their seats eight rows from the stage in the concert hall, and together they eyed the majestic, ten-foot, ebony Steinway grand piano waiting on stage. Soon the mother found a friend to talk with, and without her realizing it, her eight-year-old son slipped away from his seat and began exploring.

When 8:00 arrived, the house lights dimmed, and only then did the mother realize that her son had not returned to his seat. Frantically, she began to look around to find him. Suddenly the spotlights came up and everyone hushed when they saw the little boy sitting on the upholstered piano bench, innocently picking out the song, "Twinkle, Twinkle,

Little Star." The mother gasped and her hands flew to her mouth in surprised consternation.

Before she, or anyone else, could begin to retrieve her son, the master appeared on stage. He saw the innocent little piano player and quickly moved to the keyboard. As he sat down next to the little boy, he whispered, "Don't quit. Keep playing." Paderewski reached down with his left hand and began filling in a bass part. Soon, his right arm reached around the other side, encircling the child, to add a running obligato. Together the old master and the young novice held the crowd mesmerized! And this presentation got the loudest and longest ovation of the evening.

In our lives, unpolished and novices though we may be, it is the Master who surrounds us and whispers in our ear, time and time again: "Don't quit. Keep playing!" And as we do, He augments, supplements, supplies, nurtures, and gives until a life of amazing beauty is created.

Have there been times when you have been tempted to quit, to give up, to want to lay down the duties of motherhood? Sure. But hold on. There are eternal values at stake. The future of your little ones is critical.

The wonderful possibility of a mother's life is the challenge of raising each child to become a worthwhile citizen of the Kingdom of God.

MOTHER

I think it was a girlish hand,
Unlined, well-tended, when it held
At first, my clinging baby hand
In gentle grasps by love impelled.

I think it was a youthful face
That bent above me as I lay asleep,
And bright the eyes that watched
My rest, in that forgotten day.

I think it was a slender form
That bore my weight on tiring arm,
And swift young feet that watched my steps
To guide them from the ways of harm.

But years and cares have changed that form,
And face, and hand, have streaked with gray
    the hair,
Yet is the heart as full of love
As in that other day.

               —Author unknown

Proverbs 31:1-13

⚡ POWER POINT: Mother, don't give up, don't thrown in the towel just yet. The Source of your life is available for all the days of your life: the

82

good days, the bad days, and the just "plain days." Listen carefully in your soul. You will hear those special words from the Master, "My child, keep on, for I will be with you always!"

Dear Mother,

You're the sunshine
on a bright and cheery morning.
You're the refreshing smell in the air
when the rain approaches.
You're the gentle breeze that makes
the leaves and blossoms dance.
You're the good earth from which all
living things have sprung.

You are all these things, Mother,
because not only have you given life,
you have made it beautiful.
The Lord bless you, and keep you,
and make His face to shine upon you!

Other books by Robert Strand from Evergreen Press:

The Power of Fatherhood
Fathers have a tough job raising kids today, but author Robert Strand shares over 20 true stories combined with his 40 plus years of ministry to encourage dads to be all they can be.
ISBN 1-58169-095-9 96 p $5.99

The Power of Forgiving
True stories and practical instruction to help you deal with irritations, heal relational breaks, and forgive the "unforgivable."
ISBN 1-58169-050-9 96 p $5.99

The Power of Thanksgiving
Time to take inventory of your blessings and begin a new lifestyle of thanksgiving. Each Power Book has over 20 stories combined with the wisdom of the Scriptures.
ISBN 1-58169-054-1 96 p $5.99

The Power of Gift Giving
Learn how to give the intangible parts of your life and become a source of blessing to others. Each chapter can be read in five minutes, but the benefits will last a lifetime!
ISBN 1-58169-055-X 96 p $5.99

Power Books™
Buy them to give…read them to live!™

"A mother is the truest friend we have.
When trials, heavy and sudden, fall upon us;
when adversity takes the place of prosperity;
when friends, who rejoice with us
in the sunshine, desert us when troubles
thicken around us; still will she cling to us,
and endeavor by her kind precepts and
counsels to dissipate the clouds of
darkness, and cause peace
to return to our hearts."

—Washington Irving (1783-1859)